Here and There

Also by Joanna van Kool and published by Ginninderra Press
Now and Then
Sandhill Island 1975

Joanna van Kool

Here and There

Acknowledgments

With grateful thanks to Collen Keating for her invaluable advice; the New South Wales Women Writers' Network for their support; and to Ginninderra Press for their assistance – in particular Brenda Matthews for her creative and artistic imagination

To all my family, especially my husband, David

Here and There
ISBN 978 1 76109 323 4
Copyright © text Joanna van Kool 2022
Cover image: Brenda Eldridge

First published 2022 by
Ginninderra Press
PO Box 3461 Port Adelaide 5015 Australia
www.ginninderrapress.com.au

Contents

Give light and people will find the way – Ella Baker

Aunt Buddy	11
Life's Passengers	13
For Doctor Noel Rowe	14
On the death of a teenage friend	15
Bubbles: an Art	16
Departure	18
My Life's Friend, Judy	19
Joyless	20
Teenage Revolt	21

The basis for peace is respecting all creatures – Cesar Chavez

Maggie	25
Of people and pigeons	26
Of Birds and Man	27
Man and Beast	28
Car Park Crows	29
My black and white girl	30
A mouse	31
My Magpie	32
Pond Life	33
From where I sit I see…	34

After silence, that which comes nearest to expressing the inexpressible is music – Aldous Huxley

The reach of music	37
Lark Ascending	38
Images in a Bartok String Quartet	40

O, wind, if winter comes, can spring be far behind? –
Percy Bysshe Shelley

Rebirth	45
September	46
Springtime Wet	47
The Sounds of Spring	48
Survival	49

Difficulties are things that show what men are –
Epictetus

Difficulties	53
Misunderstood	54
Shame	55
Letting off Steam	56
Answering the difficult question	57
Disabled	58
Schizophrenia	60
A response	61
A Fear	62
Aged Care	64
Exposed	66
Isolation	67
Covid Nineteen	68
Toxicity	69
Terror	70

Never fear to deliberately walk through dark places, for that is how you reach the light on the other side –
Vernon Howard

Ullapool, Scotland	73
Amsterdam Galleries	75
A different light	76
A bush path near the city	77

Wendy Whiteley's Garden	78
A Wild Flower Garden	79
Scattered Images	80
A Drive Past	81
Adolescence	82
Bush Fire	83
Dadirri-Gwandalan	84
Listen!	85
A Sydney Fog	86

Imagination encircles the world – Albert Einstein

Some Small Images	89
Searching for more	90
Finding Him	91
Perhaps God is…	92
Creating Shapes	93
Equality	94
Clouds	95
Life in the Pond	96
A lesson in preservation	97
Unchanging	98
In Childhood	99
Cleansing Moments	100
Near Death Experience	101
Descent Into Sleep	102
Life in rocks	103
Sydney Real Estate	105

Give light and people will find the way
— Ella Baker

Aunt Buddy

The aunt I never was allowed to see
became the symbol of that other world
from which I had to be cocooned it seemed.
'You couldn't go to visit her, my dear,
the house is full of cats and crows and smells.
two crows and twenty cats – or was it more –
I just forget. I know it was quite foul –
they live in any place they choose and curl
up even in the bathroom if it's warm.
quite unhygienic, dear.
Her husband, Mont, a dreadful man;
runs a kind of garage – they never have
two bob to rub together it appears.
Oh, no, my girl, it wouldn't do at all
for you to visit her,' my granny said.
And so it was I never got to see
that aunt – 'Lady of the Cats'
who loved all living things and couldn't kill
or drown a kitten even if she starved herself.

All thoughts of her were lost
in teenage years
but then on turning twenty-one I received
a package in the mail. A tiny box
which held white tissue paper tightly screwed
around a lumpy shape – a rose gold ring –
two opals and a pearl – quite clearly old.
And when I searched for clues as to who had
sent this lovely thing I found a note
still wedged inside the envelope,

neat copperplate with downward strokes
of slightly shaky old-age hand the words
'Congratulations, dear, for this
your special day. From Aunt Buddy. With love.'

In London, student hedonistic days
left little room for thoughts of school or home
so far away, until a phone call came
and Mother said she'd be in town
and could I meet her for a chat
and coffee after class. 'Oh, yes,'
an added afterthought
'your great aunt Buddy died last week.
Can you believe it? Had a heart attack
while she was sitting
with a rabbit on her lap.
it must have been a shock
for bunny, I should think.'

That night I took
from out a drawer
the tiny ring and put
it on my little finger where it spoke
of just how much I'd missed and let pass by.

Life's Passengers

We met in sunshine near the beach
    at a restaurant called C'est Bon
where nearby gulls pranced and children squealed
    we sank into brightly cushioned chairs

Cobweb lined with age
    she bubbled enthusiastic warmth
remonstrating with her diminishing world.
    When she was ill, she said,
laughing all the while,
    she worried she might not make the journey
across the road for a carton of milk
    wondered if she'd make it back

memories wrapped like an old cloak
    around her, a life well lived
if one can call it that
    at least a life
as together we laughed
    over moments shared
remembered minute details
    could see and hear those times
again in all their sunlit brilliance

while, on the horizon
    the outline of a ship
    a black pencilled shape
    appeared to ominously wait

For Doctor Noel Rowe

Were you scared? Did you ask, why me?
I try to imagine how it must have been
but I'm not you and didn't know you well
except as a kind and gentle man
who opened a door for me
and helped me find a way with words
so now I move two steps forwards and slide back one
as ideas flow, an undammed stream.

Hearing you were sick it seemed unfair
for someone who had given that joy
and freed the pages of the soul
I sometimes lie in the early hours
to wonder how you must have felt
as death approached
Was God there with you? Did you believe?
How shall I be when the abyss yawns?
        But that's not something even you could teach.

On the death of a teenage friend

Little things I remember
       like how she pressed a tissue
              between red lips
to blot lipstick
       before applying again.
              The lines round her eyes
became screwed up
       when she laughed
which was often and made her shake.

Then she met an American
       fell in love, was married in months
             flying off to live in the States
where her life was quite
       unimaginable for me
from a photo of desert with a lone gas station
       next to motel and giant cactus.

Two lives – hers and mine
shared once in our teens
       in the excitement of London
bright full of promise
       believing our dreams
             would be fulfilled
and maybe they were
but in quite different ways

not as we planned things at all.

Bubbles: an Art

High-heeled smart she waves;
swishes between tables – flops
        Oh God, I need a drink
        George, darling, bubbly, please – you know
        the kind I always have
cute pout-smile – flash of teeth
turns back to me
        now do tell, what have you been at?
        I'm totally exhausted.
        Nick has just announced he needs to
        get away for three days golf
tight lipped – inward breath
        of course it's fine for them
        to trot off when they need a change
        but we women have to carry on,
        don't we, darling? I mean to say
        we're – *winked innuendo* – always on call.
        I sometimes wish I had a husband
        who wasn't quite so energetic
        success has its price you know
        but I seem to be the one…
smile flash at waiter
        Oh, just a little salmon
        I do try to keep the weight off
        but so many dinners we attend
        these days make the waist line grow.
        I've warned Nick if I weigh any more
        I'll need a whole new wardrobe

Leaning forward – sotto voce
>I dare not tell him I've bought
>two fab outfits this week

Another pout – toss of hair
>Well he likes me to look my best
>thank God I've got his visa card
>in my wallet, darling.

Sees me at last
>Now tell me when did we last meet?
>More champagne? On days like this
>I think – I'd die without it
>just perfect in this heat
>…'

Departure

He'd requested a humanist service,
had planned it in months of great pain.

We sat at the front of the chapel
knowing how hard it would be.

All attempts at relations were done
for this sadly unloved man

whom we'd come to know just a bit
in those last dreadful weeks

understood how he'd felt;
had viewed life all those years,

twisted and scarred at age seventeen
lifting suffering men onto stretchers

as guns ricocheted, bringing death
to all on sand hill or plain.

Eulogies read and chosen songs played,
as the final strains died,
a thistledown seed in the light of the day
floated over us all
and I knew he had stayed
for my whispered farewell.

My Life's Friend, Judy

You've been around and around all my life;
    since I was ten; forever, in my scheme of things
and I can't fully accept you've gone
    but know although time will pass
and the pain will ease
    my world will still have a gap
a space between stitches in the hems
    of tunics we wore all those years ago
when the future looked bright for us both
    and promised everything:
that was a world for which men fought
    not knowing then how things would change.

You loved, learned, became wise and kind
so my memories of you help fill the empty space
your passing leaves behind.

Joyless

Thin and bearded, there's nothing about him
        that invites a chat.
It seems he cannot smile, or if he does,
        it's just a mirthless stretch of mouth, no warmth.
Perhaps he's had some kind of breakdown
        and hasn't picked up life enough
to join the world again.
        His fingers are tobacco-stained,
though now at least he goes outside to smoke,
        sits on a low brick wall around a tree.
He works seven days in his jam-packed place
        the Two Dollar Shop
though little now is quite so cheap. His breath sighs
        'I don't care. I'm only here to make a crust,'
but I'd like to see some laughter lines around his eyes.

Teenage Revolt

'I've read your diary,' she says.
'You would, you bitch,' I think
But I say, 'So…?'
She holds it out so I can see the page
but can't read the words
though I suspect it's where I wrote
'We fucked.'
'None of your business anyway,' I say
hating her knowing smirk.
I'll bet she's jealous, wishes she
was seventeen again
when she had smart tits,
small waist and skinny hips.
'I'm disgusted,' she says
'I thought you had more depth.
It reads just like a girlie mag.'
Good, I think, *I'm glad you don't know my world
will never feel how great it is.*
Then when she turns to leave the room
I rip out the page she just defiled
by reading and throw the screwed up
paper on the floor,
               but part of me
               is wishing she would show
               some understanding in her eyes.

The basis for peace is respecting all creatures

– Cesar Chavez

Maggie

I turned from the sink and there he was
head on one side claws spread on the floor

Did he know the cats were on the bed
asleep and unaware? We stared at each other
for a moment before I went to the fridge
for the box of food and he patiently waited
      knew what I was about I'm sure
but I directed him outside to the table
to put out the lump of beef he likes
will take to his young who sometimes
      come with him now to learn the ropes
still fledglings, speckle-feathered,
sex undetermined for me as yet
when grown each will be either pure white
on the neck or mottled which means
      she's a she and less brave than he

and I was scared he might come when the cats
are awake, but I probably needn't be worried
as he knows so much more than imagined
by a human like me. He must think I'm
      a lumbering bird who sings flat songs
      unlike his musical call to his mate or child
      as he flies so free in the wild

Of people and pigeons

So many weird and off beat souls
    walk with purpose down city streets
fat-bellied man with a million tattoos
    a woman bent almost in half
thin hair no teeth drags shopping cart
    mutters to passing parade
or the young who half-run
    have clear skin and bright eyes
see the world with the wonder of youth

pigeons are just the same in a way
    run at times then go slow
like the old woman who mutters
    they make their who-whoos
then waddle with puffed-out chests
    like the fat man with tattoos

Of Birds and Man

Silhouetted against grey sky the small beak
        opens in expectation as mother bird
              leaves to forage and seek
some food for her hatchling
            too small to fly from nest
      of spit and twigs
      but quite unsafe as the wind blows cold
and rain makes it hard
for the chick to find comfort and hold
            fast in its swaying home, but it knows
its mother will come
      as her wish to protect is innate

and I think of young children huddled in tents
        pegged out in sand among flies and heat
            in countries that take them in
                everywhere but not here
      because we don't want more mouths to feed
let others worry not us for we own this land
and don't want to share
even with those who were here
aeons before we arrived and besides such souls
            might harm us cause havoc
make us less safe unlike the nest in the tree
        that tosses but stays with the trust of a bird.

Man and Beast

we know from their eyes and their cries
when they're beaten or kicked
they are sentient beasts
though they cannot talk as we do
it's their eyes or tail not their mouths that speak
when a tail gives a twitch it's speech of a kind.
We give them human abilities
call them names like our own
ones we find funny or mad
we can't understand their ways
as we're sure they don't understand
and while we acknowledge their sense
of smell is greater than ours
we think in our arrogance they don't see like us
or taste their food as we do
and when they're physically abused we convince
ourselves they feel almost nothing at all.

Car Park Crows

In the school car park
the crows gossip in nearby trees
questions and answers scratch the air
in drawn out unintelligible words
creating looping lines of black
the rise and fall of sounds tease
the listener so these yellow-eyed birds
become old ladies telling shocking tales
eliciting similar response of Awww
from neighbour leaning on the fence
mockeries of suburban chats
between bored women who crave
some excitement in their daily lives.

My black and white girl

It took some time to get her into the car
      body spread on the floor, chin just able to rest
on the seat so her brown eyes gazed at me as I drove.
      The vet said, 'Only choice is to amputate,'
but I knew there really was no choice.
      A moment of silence as I took in the facts
this creature I'd loved, fought, walked with down trails
      she following wherever I went
lay at my feet on a rug, love mixed with hairs.
      'I'll just give her something to make her relax.'
Within minutes she lay as I stroked
      her ears of silk and told her it was all right,
when it wasn't for her or for me.
      Then the needle's last thrust
and she raised one eyebrow.
      What did she say?
Whatever it was, she trusted me still
      a confirmation of her undying love
and my overwhelming sense of guilt.

A mouse

I found a baby mouse today
in gutter of six-lane highway
    where had it come from?
    Was its mother around?
I wondered what to do
knew I couldn't leave it there.
A tissue from my purse
I hoped was soft enough
to lift it from its bed of leaves
and place it in a doorway
so no car or man could stamp
upon its tiny frame.
My bus arrived and as we left
    I looked at where I'd placed
    the tiny creature to be safe
realising too late it was at the door
of the biggest brothel in the place
I then could only pray those tales
of kind Madams would prevail.

My Magpie

I envy the birds that fly
        in circling shrieks above
slicing the evening sky
        to perch on roofs or in trees.

My magpie comes at dusk
        to sit on the balcony rail
head perched on one side
        sharp beak thrust out to catch
the meat I throw in lumps
        and if I'm slow to respond
he throws back his head
        to sing as only a magpie can,
the warbling cry that comes
        from somewhere deep in his throat.
Then he waits again for me
        head cocked once more
to watch with one yellow eye.

Sometimes he looks quite cross
        when I finally go to the door.
I think mine is his last port of call
        at night before he returns
to his perch on a branch or a roof.

I tell him I won't let him down
        which I think he actually knows
but he likes to make sure I don't
        before cutting the air once more
with the speed of a black and white dart.

        wish I could see what he sees
        could move with his graceful speed

Pond Life

flags of blue water iris rise
        against the sky as goldfish
slide and jerk among water lily leaves
        green plates that sway and heave
in pond's secret dark where aquatic life
        swirls among the weeds
and tiny voice of green small frog
        tells that all is well
and life pulsates in mud and bog
        below the level water mark

From where I sit I see…

rippling green with highlights of gold
    in morning shimmering sun
spring quiver against the blue
    as amber-eyed black and white magpie
poised on balcony rail burbles
    his welcome to morning, anxiously waits
white snickering beak pointed aloft
    ready to snap catch blood rich meat
flick wrist thrown in calculated arc
    against clear and empty turquoise sky
before he dives deep down among the roofs
    and peeping chimneys as I stand
to watch and see he's perched
    to smack his beak-filled lumpy prey
on overlapping red brick tiles
    then he slices the air in his own arc
to bunch of twigs among the leaves
    where small mouths greedily grab
with clicking joyful cheeps
    and gorged they momentarily sleep
so he can return to perch again
    on balcony rail while slivering summer leaves
watch in green gold morning light.

After silence, that which comes nearest to expressing the inexpressible is music
– Aldous Huxley

The reach of music

Words have limits, constraints
even when we carefully place each piece
picture   emotion   thought
to create a believable whole
               but music lifts, moves inwards
               touches that place
               which some may call the soul.

Lark Ascending

Ralph Vaughan Williams

A clear single throated call begins
        before rising with tremulous ascent
towards the clouds spread in white
        swirled magnificence, curling to billow
through pull of azure emptiness.
        Wings tremble as the bird's joy sings
a constant full-throated high-pitched song
        to the new day's golden dawn.

He comes to rest at last in green
        whispering twist of hawthorn hedge
behind the fence of dry stone wall
        where small snail creeps to hide in crack
between the limestone crunch of stones.
        Ivy climbs the bank where pink foxgloves
start their heavenward summer stretch
        and violets dim their seasonal winking blue

Later the ocean calls its shushing roar
        so the bird flies on still with trilling song
now low enough to view sea-pinks nod in shore-line field
        and waving Queen Anne's lace that stands,
white filigree of daintiness,
        high above warm summer's grassy green
while waves suck at edge of golden sand
        spread out beyond the frowning cliffs

The birds' wings flutter over the scene
>	to dip and weave before slicing an arc
touching the tip of a bracken frond
>	in his search for nest of spittle twigs
that's safe at home through glowing dark
>	when starlit skies shine on through avian night
and for a while all is still and only a gentle breeze
>	shuffles the leaves of distant trees

till soft and early morning light
>	stirs the tawny feathered bird to lift his head
sense the dew-lit coming of the diamond dawn
>	and preen in readiness to fly in soaring arc
above the clumping green with lilting song
>	of joyous welcome to the wondrous world
lifting higher to the swirling air until he flies
>	to fold at last in heaven's luminescent skies.

Images in a Bartok String Quartet

Lined, high-cheekboned face
    hair caught behind sun-faded scarf,
Hungarian woman
    bends to secure a stook of yellow corn
while men with garlic breaths,
    silhouetted in sweat-soured shirts,
toss sheaves with pitchforks
    beneath summer storm-laden skies
and a draught horse plods bell harnessed
    between fields and up a long dirt road.

In front of low stone buildings,
    with roofs that need repair,
children squeal in play
    as an old woman stands at an open door,
wipes her hands on soiled white apron
    sucks at a gap between front teeth
watches,
    laughs,
        then calls
so the children stop their game
to look at her before they too laugh
then turn to play again.

In early night water lilies fold
        in pink sleep and grasshoppers screech
their untuned single-stringed violins
among the whispering grasses by deep lake.
Pine trees stand, stiff sentinels, against a navy sky
        their clean smell drifts from the dark wood
to where continual munch of horses
in stable dark
        creates a comforting refrain.

O, wind, if winter comes, can spring be far behind?

– Percy Bysshe Shelley

Rebirth

Streaks of purple and pink between the white
of early morning light
pencilled bright through green of bunching leaves
dapple my tread on asphalt path.
Footfalls of sun-sparkled delight.
>Plane tree branches puff and dance
>before the breeze becomes a fluted song
>round seeds hide in whispering foliage
>new life burgeoning
>as solitary flag of green
>spins and weaves to its quiescent rest.

Further off the view of blue
curves through kaleidoscope of homes
tumbling from higher ground
to almost dip their toes among the fish
waiting unseen at water's edge
>and tiny ruffles lap the bank
>with tender licks to calm the pulsing
>thread of new exhilarated life.

September

Wisteria tendrils uncurl reach across
to etch their drooping mauve
against sky's spring haze
and fiddlewood's red out-of-season leaves
hide twig basket
held together with spit
of mating currawongs
but my thirst for the indefinable
excitement of spring
is still unfulfilled.

Springtime Wet

Wind bedazzled buffeting against the grey
of a wet spring sky as clouds race
across distant horizon and multicoloured roofs
of the city where giraffe cranes stand
over Parramatta and beyond
the lumps of mountains are waves
formed from volcanic thrusts
bunched now in grey blue mounds
hidden from view at times
by haze of filigree droplets
spewing from clumping drifts
of cotton wool clouds hanging above
in never ending space of emptiness

In early spring
jonquils bounce and quiver
        dazzling clumps of colour.
        Bluebells prod the green
of September's pulsing birth.
I kneel in worship to weed
        the unwanted invasion
        in spaces between.
The sun-smoothed day
        reveals tiny splats of rain
which soothed the night
        clinging still to the edge of leaves
now twinkling to wink at the day
        and hibernation now done
        the ground awakes
        with a joy freshly born.

The Sounds of Spring

Above Woolworths crows on black poles craw
      their conversations slow Aww of shock at news
pigeons hoo-hoo waddle in the park below
      and grating early morning screech of cockatoo
soars flash of white to scratch its voice
      against the blue of day as black branched trees slash
the light and Indonesian cuckoo
      mourns the brilliance with its repetitious cry
building to crescendo wail.
      Shrieking lorikeets dart in and out
excited joy of red and green
      among the shivering leaves of nearby mango tree
miniature tweets from myna bird dot
      the jasmine scented air while somewhere a dog
           barks
hiding the man-made sounds of day.

Survival

Outside the unit block in small untended patch
    the red fire hydrant stands behind the green
of bushes planted without thought no doubt
    by some council worker at some stage
who could not imagine how this would grow
    to hide the ugly tap behind its leaves
and for a while it flourished growing tall
    but finally a fireman came and saw how difficult
it was for access to water in time of fire
    so clippers came along with saw to cut away
the offending branches and throw them out
    the now small bushes shiver with cold
among ice cream wrappers and empty cans
    flung among its truncated arms
it is left to die at edge of street
    but it refuses to give up the fight
and as usual in winter small white flowers
    with centres of red blink and wink
from among leaves at the warming winter sun

Difficulties are things that show what men are
– Epictetus

Difficulties

I can only imagine how it must feel
to be from another land
with limited skills and no friends
        no money but needs like everyone
        though the language is hard
and welfare is harder
        to access with no clues as to what
        the man at the counter says in his gruff
and impersonal way.

Misunderstood

I saw the man who sells the Big Issue magazine
        on Saturdays and felt that tug of concern for those
whose lives have maybe not gone well.
        I took five dollars from my purse
saying, 'That's for you. I don't need the magazine.'
        His eyes lit up for that one second as he said
'Thank you, love,' before he pocketed the note
        and I felt good, believed I'd done something kind.
A few weeks later I saw a large black woman
        set down her pile of magazines ready to sell
to passers by at the entrance of the supermarket store,
        and I felt once more concern that tugged, so pulled
another fiver from my purse to push it in her hand.
        'For you,' I said again. 'No need for magazine.'
Her smile was one of grateful thanks and again
        I felt that flush of warmth that goes with such
a moment,
                but then I had another thought,
'How dare I take away the only thing
that's really hers,' and I wanted to go back to say
        'I'm sorry that I failed to understand
your dignity is what you need to keep,'
        and I vowed that next time I would take
her held-out magazine

Shame

When lying awake in the night
I wonder if those who condemn
others to lives of despair
are in innocent sleep

if I wake with a start
from a dreadful nightmare
hearing agonised cries
from inside a hut

or a tent in the sand
it seems some men don't care
can ignore those in pain
or perhaps are quite unaware

Letting off Steam

Sometimes anger chokes
and I'm driven to write
    another 'Dear Sir' which
helps calms the rage.
    Letters shimmer
    with furious words
to politician, councillor, someone
        who could actually help
          but won't
    when I read it again
it doesn't say what I mean at all.

The thought of a walk
to the post office makes me feel tired
    so I go sit in front of TV
    forget it all for a while

but in night's sleepless dark
I remember again and vow
to rewrite my anger
that it may be clearly understood.

Answering the difficult question

In an interview one day I was surprised
        when asked what being a Christian meant
        asked for a one-sentence response
I gave my answer then questioned
        what the interviewer would have said?
        He thought probably the same
which set me wondering
        how our leaders might respond?
        Surely it would preclude
                acting as they often do
                in ways that cannot be classed
                as based on Bible texts
the Son of God
        who loved all men
                forgave those who sinned and raised the dead
cured the sick and mentally ill
hurt no man but questioned the rights
        of those in power
perhaps the same could be asked today
of those who
        cast men aside to die
on islands where they are of no worth

Do our leaders truly believe
or
as I suspect, just mouth their creed?

Disabled

Grasping a strawberry in her tiny hand
        she carried it back
to the house and her mother
        who screeched as she saw
pink juice flow
        through three-year-old fingers,
'What have you done, you naughty girl?'

Small mouth formed
        the shape of an o
not with desire to eat or with shame
        but to capture that berried joy;
to retain the sight and smell.

Difference made others laugh
        ridicule and tease
so she retreated into her world
        which nobody else could reach.

Paint splashed across paper
        which was held up to hurt
called 'stupid' and 'rubbish'
        and though she felt shame
clung still more to her dreams.

With passing years
> all magic eventually ceased;
crushed by pressures and time
> colours were drowned in brown sludge
and thoughts were misted and hazed.

As the sunlight laughed
> through shivering leaves
words she tried to recall
> were not what she meant at all.
> When she danced with bare feet on the lawn
relatives thought she was crazed
> and shut her away from the world.

Schizophrenia

Delicate steps sway in heavy boots
befuddled and smoke-hazed
he latches onto a face
'How was your trip?' Answering words
snake hiss to writhe between
booming cars
and his demon
follows him; sees into his soul
badgers him and when he turns
his head to shout 'fuck off'
the 'thing' is still there
grinning at his angry words.

A response

On the way to make my case
to demonstrate I really cared
I sat next to a man who spoke
loudly to his friend
'No room here for bleeding hearts
look at Europe, what a mess
they haven't any idea of how to deal
with those from foreign shores
I'd tell them to fuck off.'

I know now what I should have said
but didn't at the time
I should have tuned my sweetest voice
'It's your compassion I admire.'
I might have received puzzled look
disdain at least, but maybe
I could have made a dent
in the arrogant belief
that he was absolutely right
to turn away those undeserving lesser souls
and he obviously believed
we should forget those refugees.

A Fear

The swoosh of the lift doors
before the nameless bodies
stand suspended;
minds already floors above.
A lurch!
All movement stops!
A shuffle of unease,
annoyance at this interruption
to their lives
to their planned continuation
to the floors above.
Nothing!
Personalities emerge from
inside the dress, the suit,
'Try the ground floor again.'
'Press emergency.'
Then distant microphone reply,
'Don't worry, please. It won't be long.'

With mutters of dissatisfaction
eyes covertly note
the other encapsulated souls
but when looks are caught
faces assume unruffled calm
until in a corner at the back
a moan begins,
stops
        starts again;
                a dirge of fear
as she feels lift walls
begin to close,
sting of razor,
grip of terror's vice,
pricks of red-hot needles
ice-splash on back.
The others stand embarrassed
at fear lurking in themselves,
while she slides down the wall
till, head buried, she curls
to shut out these demons of the dark.

Aged Care

She silently sits and stares into space.
Each day is the same with only colours
      outside telling of change
        if it's hot or cold, wet or dry.
The TV blares but is a meaningless sigh
of sound to her in her chair next the bed
      and no friendly face comes with talk
      of the life she once lived in her home
      in the 'burbs' with her dog that she walked
      each day to the park for a play with a ball.

Then life had meaning and purpose for her
but here the aide puts a cup in her hand
though it shakes and tea slops on her dress
as the old woman next to her laughs
with imaginary friend who's there every day
it would seem but has nothing to say
to her as she waits for the next meal
or death whichever comes first.

When a man in a suit and tie arrives
the matron who smiles as she speaks
of these 'wonderful souls' 'living well'
'given care' in this place with good food
and 'so clean' she says as she wipes her hand
over a table to show there's no dust.

They part at the door and the man
ticks the box on the form to show that he's been
to see for himself that the place is clean
so the absentee owners can still make
the money the company needs to send
to overseas tax havens so the old lady's
still cared for in this 'so caring' place
as she sits in her chair and stares into space.

Exposed

The world knows now but
he could not have known he'd be the spark
that lit the fuse of anger turned to fire
within the hearts and minds of tortured souls
who cried in pain from wounds
inflicted by a powerful union
of uniforms unanswerable
to those they hit and kicked
and those who bled on streets
or in gaol cells where unseen before
they now are heard

A phone snapped pictures
shared with friends
became the means to spread the word
so all could know the dreadful truth

everyone now heard him sob
'I cannot breathe'
as he begged to be released
millions knew what had occurred
and all white men seeing it
should no longer sleep with ease

Isolation

My world becomes smaller, shrunk in all ways
    small things are significant now like never before
the tree on the corner is losing its leaves
    and paint on the shopfront opposite peels
and falls on the footpath to be sniffed by a dog
    as it passes looking for somewhere to pee
the shift of the sun in the day can be watched
    shadows make patterns on walls that once
went unnoticed but now become part
    of my night-time dreams though day is confused
with the night and I no longer sense when to sleep.

Covid Nineteen

Now there is
    silence in all the streets nearby
walking them I see almost no one
    except maybe a young woman jogging
or purposefully walking as if she had some place
    to go when she won't have in fact
but feeling claustrophobic in her flat
    her only company a ginger cat
which she talks to as if to a close friend
    when her true close friend lives a mile away
and they can only speak on the phone each day
    in a way that makes them feel better
when I pass her she smiles
    as if we've been friends for years
which makes me think that just maybe
    it's all been worthwhile and now we
connect with each other and she really sees me

Toxicity

From my eyrie I watch the traffic's flow
    can see the whispering flutter of leaves
in plane tree above the footpath
    as moan and grind of bus and car
cause toxic fumes to rise
    I can hear man's urgent cries
but none look up to marvel at the reaching arms
    of shivering green and gold in autumn light
I want to shout 'Take heed, take heed
    this tree's worth so much more than us.'
The indigenous people know a tree's worth
    have cared for all living things
    while we have dug holes in the ground
    to satisfy greed and sullied the air we breathe.
The silhouette of branches cross the sky
    giant brooms to sweep those poisons out
but prey to whims and greed it may not survive
    so in years to come when it should still stand
it may well have been sacrificed to man.

Terror

a microscopic germ
        has been let loose
to swirl and whirl between people and lands
around the world
        cause havoc in so many ways
from panic to death
        one might be next in line
pass from this life
        alone   unable to speak   or breathe
each day pink-pronged globes
slide across TV screens
        bounce behind readers of news
        behind women and men
        who speak in grim tones

I marvel
        such a small thing
can call the world to a halt
so we shun each other in the street
        and can't speak to friends we meet
in the park
        or shake hands with those
we were taught to revere
        or at least respect
even prime ministers and presidents
        cower at the thought
they may be infected
        could possibly die
though some still believe
        they will surely be spared
        if they only pray to their God

Never fear to deliberately walk through dark places, for that is how you reach the light on the other side
– Vernon Howard

Ullapool, Scotland

A converted bothy or shepherd's hut outside Ullapool
in Scotland's far north is where I connect
with maternal ancestors I never knew.
>   Here the smell of earth and curtain of mist
>   hangs among fruit rich apple trees
>   leaning down towards the loch
>   whose dark waters flow through town
>   then out to sea and the Summer Isles

In this mystical Brigadoon of a place
the tiny birds don't sing, but simply cheep to tell
of early light or coming night time dreams
>   and twice a day the ferry slowly chugs
>   its watery way to or from the outer isles
>   past coast's grey etch of sand below the hills
>   where seals and otters chase or play
>   around the scattered driftwood washed ashore.

Here winter sleep is long and seems
this world has moved to another place
but when the spring arrives
>   the grey becomes a lighter shade and streams of smoke
>   no longer rise all day from chimneys down the hill
>   the path I tread to walk the dog is no longer mud
>   though still coldly damp from remaining winter chill
>   as heather grows again among grey stones.

I watch a snail creep up a dry-stone wall
where moss still clings to its slithery path

wintry silence is now replaced by springtime sounds.
    Below the house sheets in billowing white
        wait to catch the warmth of silvery midday sun
        and higher up the fir trees stand in ominous crowds
        awakening slowly from their winter freeze
        to whisper in the salt-soaked cleansing breeze

Amsterdam Galleries

    Rembrandt's starched white lace collars
        below glowing faces
shining with reds and yellow oils
    mixed to cleverly recreate
parchment seventeenth-century skins
    stiffly alive in heavily gilded frames

standing behind designated lines
    I feel the rich black red of velvet coats;
smell the intermingled scent of age and spice.
    Wall after wall of Dutch heaviness
        shuffling feet and quiet speech
        in dark timber-panelled solidity

Then in a different place
I discover van Gogh's
    half mad tortured mind;
    his joy of brush thick strokes
unique creation of light
    so flowers and cornfields swirl and dance
    while black crows ominously circle overhead

A different light

soft yellow light of English dawn
birds songs – scales and trills –
joyous repetitious welcome
to another happy
sun filled day

but in Australia's blaze
of brilliant light
there are no such gentle songs
just irreverent mirthful cries
as wings flap noisily in vibrant skies.

A bush path near the city

We walk the roughly created path
      rocks turned into steps with fallen branch
nearby in scrubby bush of undergrowth.
      Below the gums and nameless native trees
the glimpse of blue seems almost make-believe
      shining now from mirrored sunlit sky
when all else seems brushed with browns and greens.
      Tree trunks lean in shades of whites and greys
and leaves drip long fingers to toss their way
      with gentle flutter in early afternoon breeze.
There the white of single flannel flower
      smilingly nods in this magic hour
when ping of bellbirds prod the day
      but no other person breaks the spell
of this track above the riverside way.

Wendy Whiteley's Garden

Who would know it was built in grief?
The joyful garden spills down the hill
    a wonder of ways and plants
where trees reach skywards so that black arch
    of steel is only glimpsed between the gaps
where white or grey trunks of gums
    twist and bend to dappled light.
Palms stand proud within plain sight
    of the house and paths meander gently
past sandstone walls slowly built
    rock by rock with gift giving love
from those still tending the place
    through bird song days
and bat flying dusk when black wings flap
    above angel trumpet's lush white bells
bent low over chip bark track.
    Steps edged with railway sleepers
dragged from the rail line below
    to where visitors picnic and children run
and skip on patch of lawn or under trees.
    Time has no meaning here where all can come
to savour nature unadorned
    a promise of life renewed to all who've mourned.

A Wild Flower Garden

In a wild flower garden I breathed in the scent of gums
after summer's great fire had ravaged the place.
I stared at the many greens reaching into the light
so brilliantly bright every leaf held promise of life
miniature pink boronia nestled shyly down
white orchid's tiny blossoms thrust to the day
and brown banksia blooms reached high.
The unaccustomed quiet was so great
my breath curled at the edge of this silence
before a flock of cockatoos swirled white above
with screech and call that knifed the air
looping and weaving they left at last
and quiet returned though my shoes still crunched
dry leaves and fallen twigs,
corpses spread on the path,
all part of nature's way
incomplete and never done
a magic revelation every day.

Scattered Images

pelicans perch on posts in a row
        or beg for scraps from the café nearby
catching detritus flung from above
        by a man who stands on the wharf
they snick snack ignoring those who watch

our boat chugs past mangrove swamps
        where fishes breed in secret dark
away from man's destructiveness
        and houses are old timber shacks
or pale brick giants with ironed smooth lawns

'look at me' mansions with eyes that stare
        in supercilious emptiness
as children shriek at the sight
        of soldier crabs that staccato dance
on the edge of their watery world

A Drive Past

The house looks smart now
garage turned into master suite
windows looking onto road
garden neat out front
grassed and freshly mown
I'm told there is a pool at back
with barbecue and trampoline
family necessities it seems
but I remember a different place
when tall gum stood front and rear
and hens scratched dirt
in jacaranda's dappled light
I can hear their mutterings even now
squawking when an egg was laid
I can see my husband staking beans
or paintbrush fertilising passion flowers
piling nature's bounty by the kitchen sink
our outdoor room once housed a bat
cockatoo Augusta came each day
there must have been grey days of rain
but I remember only sun, the whole place bathed
in warmth when joyful chaos was our chosen way.

Adolescence

The dark-skinned boy swings above the creek
yells as the rope pitches him over the edge
of the water and drops him down
teeth flash bright between smiling lips
and he shouts in his own tongue to his mates
before he lets go of the rope
Splash!
Disappears into the dark river below
bubbles rise in the swirling water
and he surfaces again with a gasp
shaking his head so the drips fly
from his hair that sprays in bouncing curls
as he reaches to hold the rope once more
and swing out testing his strength
in his world of disappearing innocence

Bush Fire

a pale grey veil engulfs the world
        sting of eyes, biting smell of smoke
        darkness descends as a huge roar
                sucks and grows in rage
timber hisses as flicking heat spreads
red and yellow tongues to creep and eat
        the brush and maliciously twist up trees
so all bush creatures trying to hide
        can no longer breathe and small eyes
        mirror the gleaming flames
before frozen in fear they dim
then die with agonised cries
        even as water sprays relief
on embers' smoke in barren land

and smouldering piles of grey ash lie
        as above the trees a returning bird
cries in mournful sorrow to the sky

Dadirri-Gwandalan

House of Sacred Space

Beside the beach,
        gull-stippled yellow glare of sand
with curving water mark of wave
        serrated red-brick units;
rectangles spread as far as eye can see
        row on row;
swish on swish of passing cars;
        clatter and roar of skateboard;
sudden grating shout

it is easy to miss
        the low stone wall,
tree branch draped,
        lopsided wrought-iron gate
path with mulched brown leaves
        winds gently up past clivea beds
to where, despite the stare of unit blocks,
        which glower and frown
tranquillity persists.

Listen!

there are tiny
> whisperings at the heart of our land

little scratches
> denting our consciousness

saying we learnt nothing from those
> living here for aeons who understood

how trees grow and what they need.
> We should perhaps stand and listen

to murmuring wind through grasses
> the mournful cries of winging birds

telling us what we should know
> about survival in this land

where red dust often hides the sun
> and wide rivers may no longer flow.

Dry earth cracks and gasps
> for months before rain falls at last

and sparkling rivulets run along
> deep creases in the soil until once more

small seeds joyfully burst forth
> green harbingers of life new born.

A Sydney Fog

The white fog creeps from the valley below
spreads closed fist knuckles across the land
so the world is hidden behind a growing veil
suffocating trees and multicoloured brick
of buildings so they've been stamped out
when they normally stand like tall
giants against a sky of puff ball clouds

At last the white begins to lift
and the wintry sun breaks through
to reveal the land beyond our home
where spread-out buildings crowd
into the distance once more
and the river winds its way through
that quilted patchwork view.

**Imagination encircles the world
– Albert Einstein**

Some Small Images

1

In separate bed
I miss the warmth of silky skin
your breath in my hair.

2

When he turned and walked
away, part of him remained
suspended in air.

3

        With sails raised in the breeze of open sea
        we lean and fly.
        Wind sucks and canvas slaps tight
        as we slice through blue magnificence.

4

    We were
seeds sown too early
    contorted, struggled
flowered briefly
    so bees near missed us
autumn wind lifted
    spent heavy heads
soft seed sun drifting
    spoke wistful goodbyes.

Searching for more

reaching beyond
        the white rabbit's burrow
for something new, different
        quite crazy, but a clear
choice of words that speak
        to others conveying
images of patchwork vibrancy
        that seem now unattainable
I stretch my fingers
        over labelled computer keys
sniff the air for perfumed sounds
        hear the secretly whispered scene
taste the joy of moving
        beyond known limitations
to recreate the familiar
        in my own independent voice.

Finding Him

Gold flash from sensor as incense rises
                snake-swirl against blue stained glass
    He is not here.
Stone arches, built to worship
                the magnificent glory of God
    He is not here.

Among dry stones on red earth
                a lizard darts bright-eyed
rain drops hang from suspended leaf
                kiss of life for a bee.

In that hurtful heat
                threading the silence

        here may He be heard

Perhaps God is…

not a benign being, not female or male
        neither black nor white but a very pale
rainbow coloured essence that flows
        like a flood over desert and dry land
        seeps into crack and folded crease
        into song of magpie and currawong
        into the making of war and peace.
It cannot be seen but is always in view
plays no part in our lives but is life itself
        to be savoured and suffered by those
        who travel the roads of joy and pain.
This quiddity continues to creep
        down rivers that run to the sea
live in the soil or fly with grey and white clouds
        that like puffballs sweep through the air
and it is needed by all that grows
with or without our being aware.

Creating Shapes

There's a lady in the gum outside my window
        wide shouldered, silent, reaching for the blue
                to dance and wave to the world
her whispers echo through the leaves
        and way above, her face
                is lost awhile among green swaths
so I can't know if it's joy or screams of pain
she shouts to the wild wind's rage.

Equality

Long-gone voices told tales so our futures
       were set; religion or culture proclaimed
where we stand in terms of power
       the creator was male, came to earth in male form
though his mother was allowed some importance.
She met with angels and God we're told in words
       of beauty but sadly translations so we really
don't know what they meant at that time
       aeons ago when few were literate
but still asked the same questions we ask today
Is there a God? Where do we go after Death?
       And given stock answers people
       accepted the wisdom nearly always from men.

If women demanded their rights they were punished
       burned at the stake or locked up in that place
called Bedlam for daring to challenge
       the male-decreed roles.

Now we're making the change at last
but some make it a difficult task.

Clouds

Islands of clouds hover and fluff
their hundred puffballs blown in globes
softly float in wait for wind
to carry them north over the red
and yellow furnace gobbling the land
in urgent rage a fevered pandemic
among the trees and tangled scrub
the withheld wet those bundled white
shapes hold in tear drops
so fine they are unseen
and gather in myriad images to whisper
among the blue of heaven's nothingness

Life in the Pond

orange flash and swirl mouths open to gulp they
twist through lily pads sitting above the gloom
stems reach down into the depths where
neither moon nor sunlight reach
dragonfly dances across the shine
of water pleated now by breeze
leaf flutters from contorted trunk
of liquidambar ages old
the tiny croak of miniature frog
leaves behind its wriggling slipperiness
struggles to climb the Everest of slime
to where life calls insistently
with pleasurable bubble pops
near scent of purple lily flower

> but fear still lurks from dark grey shapes
> winging above in daylight brilliance

A lesson in preservation

Green gloom of tangled place
        empty of all but weeds
surely nothing lives where once a hoya grew
in hanging basket hidden from view.

        But then a tendril of a plant appears
reaching it seems to find safe space
        I trace the source, discover tiny roots
have sunk into bark of nearby tree

Without disturbing others
        nature demonstrates, like man,
the need to find somewhere safe
        to grow and ultimately breed.

Unchanging

The tree on the corner stands unchanged
except for its leaves of orange and brown
lying now on footpath in crackling piles
children shuffle and toss them in air
but the tree is totally unaware of how we live
now in our fear of the virus reaching out
to grab our throats and lungs when we get too close
in café or crowded grocery shop
and its branches sweep across sunlit blue
caught in the now and unafraid but surely aware
death in its twirling leaves will inevitably come
before the force that drives all life is reborn
through seeds that shoot in springtime sun

In Childhood

I knew what heaven was like and how rain came.
    It was from the coffee percolator's glass ball
where water dripped into grains below,
    only the rain's glass globe was huge.
Heaven was in the clouds above somewhere;
    things were simpler and innocent then.
Everyone was nice, even old Aunt Kate
    whose hearing trumpet frightened me;
even the man at the beach who shouted
    when I patted his dog with sandy hands.
Everything was bright blue, green or red;
    days and months were always colours
Tuesday was pale blue, Sunday emerald green
    December was red like the berries of holly
and mistletoe looked like small balls of milk
    hanging low down in the hall.
When visitors came they kissed us
    below where it swung from the light.
That's where I got my first proper kiss
    from a boy much older than me.

    It was not as I thought it would be!

Cleansing Moments

We drip in February heat to wade through heaviness
of crowds blurred in noise of radiant summer light
dream-like shimmers of midday sun under hats
that bob and bounce down busy city streets
looking for the cool of dappled shade
when in a moment of sheer surprise
fast moving clouds envelope light
and breezes tease the body's sweat
momentary gasps of sheer relief
before a single drop of rain splats on path
followed by another till intermittent drips
make dots on grey cement and people start to move
with light tread and energy is renewed.
Each rain spot smacks on arms and neck
cold wet shocks on burning skin
as dry earth sucks the water in
beseeching trees reach out for speck
of spluttered unexpected wet
gutter rubbish swirls and sweeps down drains
and all seems completely cleansed.

When the rain stops at last we shake ourselves
and struggle back along the street
in draining February heat.

Near Death Experience

I found myself staring down a straight path
running between autumnal trees
where branches flamed with coloured leaves
of orange and yellow and some bright reds
as my shoes crunched those fallen in drifts
which someone it seemed had swept to the side
so the path-in front cut like a spear through the wood.
I stood for a while to take in the scene
which seemed brighter than any I'd known before.
I became conscious then of someone else
who stood quite close, but I couldn't quite see
in some strange way and for an unknown reason.
I couldn't ask him or her to show themselves
but it was all quite calm and I felt
at peace with this companion who didn't speak
and made no sound as we walked side by side
down the sunlit colourful tree-lined path.
When I stopped, the stranger did too
so for a second I thought I should feel fear
but I sensed only warmth and knew this
was a being I could trust with my life
though we didn't talk, but continued to walk
in companionable silence to some unknown place.

After a time it seemed we'd arrived at a point
the stranger knew, but I did not and when I turned
my head to speak at last, there was no one in sight
and I felt a great void where my new friend had been
but as the bright light dimmed I felt quite certain
when I opened my eyes I'd see a white ceiling
and the now familiar hospital curtains

Descent Into Sleep

Eyes close to shut out light
    before entering forest of pine
        where no whisper of wind
shivers the quiet
and leaves lie thick on ground
    so starts
        the slow
            sinking
                down
                into that growing dark.
But a thought,
a momentary spark
    pierces the silent escape from time
        brings back the world from space
to be relived in slow motion
    with colours swirling in joy mixed with shame
        for guilt is embedded in every frame
of recalled years past – unheeded cry of pain
    gesture of love unremarked
        then tossing begins amid rustling wind
so for a while the forest is lost
but the trees reach out once more
    as stillness at last
        embraces the dark

Life in rocks

I

There's a cutting in the rock
      where a seed found a small hole
in a crack where no one could
      see no man could poison
or even cared if it grew or died
      it received little sun
but the rain dripped steadily
      into its bed of dark sleep
so it soon uncurled
      reached out to the light,
and each time I drive
      through the tunnel of rock
I salute the waving plants
      demonstrating their defiance

2

A trickle ran
> steadily from a crack
in the sandstone
> and people lined up in cars
and waited with cans
> or bottles for filtered water
so pure it was how I imagined it
> must have been long ago
in biblical times
> but some official men
plastered the crack
> so no one could see
or taste the cold freshness
> share any more the delight

Sydney Real Estate

A striking castle is advertised for sale
expecting countless millions in the bids.
It sounds interesting so we decide to visit
drive to where it stands, imposing sandstone,
overlooking one end of Sydney harbour up a creek
very grand indeed but hidden well
behind a hedge and various trees
so privacy is still maintained for the man who buys
this priceless piece of vintage Sydney circa 1895

then we drive to see another smaller house
two bed one bath a deceased estate we read
it looks a mess, in dire need of TLC
which I'm too old now to give and don't have
the money anyway,
        but if I did I'd love to buy that little home
        much more me than a grand old mansion built of stone.

www.ingramcontent.com/pod-product-compliance
Lightning Source LLC
Chambersburg PA
CBHW050302120526
44590CB00016B/2463